TEACHERS
AND
STUDENTS

Honoré Victorin Daumier

DAUMIER AND THE UNIVERSITY

TEACHERS

AND

STUDENTS

PREFACE, CATALOGUE AND NOTES

BY

RAYMOND PICARD

PROFESSOR AT THE SORBONNE

BOSTON BOOK AND ART, PUBLISHER

BOSTON, MASSACHUSETTS

Translated from the French by Arnold Rosin
Library of Congress Catalog Card Number 74-124158

A SUBJECT OF CONTEMPORARY SIGNIFICANCE

WAS Daumier involved in the great arguments of the time about school and university education? Yes and no, it seems. It is certainly true that when, towards the end of 1845 and during the first half of 1846, he published in *le Charivari* the plates which form the series *Teachers and Students,* he did not remain indifferent to the problems of the educational system which were among the most discussed questions of the time. But in fact it must be made clear at the outset that though he denounces a certain number of abuses and absurdities of school life, he does not seem to have intended taking up the debate in its full scope. In a study on *l'Écolier* published in 1841 in *les Français peints par eux-mêmes,* which is really a sociological inquiry before its time, the writer observes that the schoolboy, "systematically maintains a struggle against authority, a struggle as full of hate and as relentless as that of the Guelfs and the Ghibellines, which carries on uninterrupted from generation to generation. The pupil brings to bear all his lack of submission, his cantankerousness, his vexatious mockery, his intransigence, while the teacher responds with all the authority he has been granted and by the blind prodigality with which he delivers *pensums, retenues* and *mauvais points.*" Daumier limits himself to presenting the revengeful pictures of this eternal war between schoolboys on the one hand and teachers and supervisors on the other, "a constant struggle between masters and schoolboys," as Balzac described it in *Louis Lambert,* "a struggle with no quarter given, which has no comparison in society apart from the battle of the Opposition against the Ministry in a representative government." With his horror of power whatever its form and his love of liberty in every field, we have no difficulty in surmising Daumier's attitude, but beyond this old libertarian anarchism which characterizes him, it

5

seems obvious that it stems from no system whatever, no partisan position, not even from any very precise opinion.

Daumier's choice of subject is in any case easy to explain. In many instances, we laboriously ask ourselves why, at a particular time, the caricaturist chose to deal with one theme rather than with another, but here the reply is quite clear. He allowed himself to be guided by current preoccupations. The satirical daily newspaper, le Charivari, published in each issue a full-page lithograph which formed its chief attraction. Daumier, its most distinguished caricaturist, found his subject matter in a field which had been the object of intense scrutiny for several months past, namely, that of education. There was a great deal of vigorous dispute raging at the time about the whole question of schools, and the quarrels found an echo in the columns of le Charivari itself. Daumier's plates therefore appeared in a very special ideological and political climate of opinion, which must be re-created, even if it finally emerges that this atmosphere offered the artist a vague point of departure rather than a specific source of ideas.

The battle against the State monopoly in education had been raging since 1843. Napoleon had in principle entrusted the State with all responsibility for education. In fact, however, in the *Rapport au Roi sur l'Instruction secondaire* of 1843, we read that public schools, royal and secondary schools then numbered some 70,000 students, whereas private institutions and boarding schools contained almost 35,000. Certainly a fraction of the last named attended courses in the *collèges,* but on the other hand there were almost 20,000 pupils in ecclesiastical institutions and in *petits séminaires.* A good number of them, for whom dancing and fencing lessons were organized, were not destined for the Church. Well over one-third of all pupils were therefore in private schools and the State monopoly had become nothing more than a meaningless concept. Even so, free education was being campaigned for with unabated vigor, and the Catholic newspaper, *l'Univers,* was especially notable in this campaign. Although the Government accorded ever more concessions, the clergy, as the *Histoire populaire contemporaine* was to remind its readers twenty years later, "demanded absolute liberty and stated that the State had no right to teach. It proved it theoretically by establishing that the State, having no State religion and therefore no doctrine, could offer merely an atheistic form of instruction, and it attempted to prove this by nominally carrying on war against the most eminent university professors such as Victor Cousin, Théodore Jouffroy, Jules Simon and Damiron. But the more violent protagonists did not stop there; they sought to uncover each teaching crime in the State educational system and every conceivable horror in its *collèges* which they called pestilential schools. The principle of *liberté d'enseignement* was taken up by several newspapers of the liberal opposition, who followed the clergy, while failing to understand that, in a country

6

such as France in which the clergy is the only body with considerable personnel and great resources, if the State ceased to teach, the clergy would teach entirely by itself. This was their true goal."

To this offensive of the clergy against the University one sector of public opinion responded by violent attacks on the Jesuits who had been prohibited in France since their expulsion and the suppression of their Company under the ancien régime. However, they had re-established themselves and regained great influence during the Restoration. "A very curious result of this struggle," continues the *Histoire populaire contemporaine,* "was the revelation of the presence in France of the Jesuits." The Government was asked to account for their failure to execute the laws. It replied that it had not noticed the Jesuits. They had settled in the Rue des Postes (now the Rue Lhomond), and this principal house had several annexes in the provinces. Public opinion was violently moved by this news, especially when Michelet and Quinet vigorously attacked the Jesuits in lectures on the Inquisition and the Jesuits from the rostrum at the Collège de France." As early as 1843 passions were unleashed. Many demonstrations occurred in the Latin Quarter only to be brutally suppressed, and as often happens, innocent strollers were struck down by the police. In December 1845 when Daumier's plates were beginning to be published, *le Charivari* suggested "digging tunnels beneath the Latin Quarter branching out in every direction, so that non-student pedestrians might reach their destination and go about their business in entire safety below street level, while people above were being stabbed and beaten to within an inch of their life."

In Parliament as well as in the newspapers and in the streets, the educational problem was debated to such a degree that on February 26, 1846 in announcing publication of *l'Abbé Aubin,* a short story by Prosper Mérimée, *le Constitutionnel* is careful to state that it is concerned, "neither with the University nor with the Jesuits." The reforms decided upon were debated with great vigor. The *rétribution universitaire* (expenses of day pupils) was suddenly increased from sixty to a hundred francs, and *le Charivari* observed, "this is a strange way to make us understand the cost of education!" The composition of the Royal Commission on Education, at that time very influential, was modified. "The public," *le Charivari* observed, "should be greatly concerned whether it is the Council of Eight or that of Thirty which wears the caftan of the University pasha, whether it is Monsieur Salvandy (the Minister) or Messieurs Saint-Marc Girardin, Dubois, Cousin and others who have the poor teachers coming and going like slaves." This was merely a passing expression of sympathy, for as a rule *le Charivari* had little compassion for teachers, being more prone to deride their pedantic and incorrect language and reproach them for their absenteeism (for at the time they had the right, often abused, of turning their teaching duties over to substitutes, while themselves retaining an important proportion of their salary). Daumier's newspaper also criticized the exam system, though it is true that it was not a question here of university exams. "Those who present themselves for mere office jobs and posts as expeditionaries in the War Department have to take oral und written exams. It seems that one is much less demanding when it comes to appointing the minister himself." In essence, *le Charivari* appears to have shared the attitude of the organs of the liberal opposition, as mentioned by *Histoire populaire*. "The State," it declared, "should not enjoy a monopoly in the field of education . . . rather, it should thoroughly reorganize, on the one hand its teaching body, which is the University and on the other its supervisory body responsible for deciding conflicts within the teaching profession, namely, the Ministry of Public Instruction."

SCHOOL LIFE AS PORTRAYED BY DAUMIER

What was Daumier's personal attitude to the problem? With his ability to gauge public interest, he was at once aware of the advantages of turning to a problem which was then one of the most widespread public preoccupations. But in what spirit did he deal with it and at which level? We must note at the outset that in all these plates there is not the slightest allusion to the Jesuits, nor to the Royal Commission, nor to the *rétribution universitaire*. Nor is there anything to indicate a fixed point of view on the question of the State monopoly: a certain number of scenes occur in boarding schools or private institutions, yet others can quite well be situated in State *collèges*; the artist does not seem to have bothered making any careful distinction. In fact, it appears that he wanted to benefit from the vogue of the theme without giving it any precise political significance. The value of the theme lay for him not so much in the quarrels it provoked at the time as in its human value and graphic potential.

We merely have to pay attention to the meaning he gave it in the title itself, *Teachers and Students*. A text of *les Français peints par eux-mêmes* (1841) gives a useful definition of the word *moutard* in the French title of the series *Professeurs et Moutards (Teachers and Students)*. It was not only a common and imprecise synonym for "child" or "youngster." In the schools we are told, "power usually belongs to the eldest and is based on how advanced pupils are, so that it becomes porportionally greater higher up the school." Thus the older pupils consider themselves aristocrats. "These proud patricians," writes Henri Rolland in *l'Écolier*, "regard the entire common people around them as *moutards* or brats *(mômes)*; they extort from them and abuse their power with unbridled despotism." The kids portrayed by Daumier are often first form pupils

—the caption of plate 15 says so specifically—and above all the upper classes of the primary department annexed to the schools, the second and the top forms. The caricaturist does not show students following Michelet's lectures at the Collège de France nor pupils in the fifth and sixth forms.

Similarly, instead of introducing the teachers of the upper classes, who after all are more representative of secondary teaching, he turned to those who, in the educational process, came immediately after the elementary teachers. They taught the youngest classes and were at the time known as *régents*. Better still, Daumier's teachers are often mere supervisors. Under such conditions, the artist could scarcely be involved in the political questions surrounding education. These lithographs are part of a social satire but not properly speaking of a political satire.

Scholastic organization and its functioning are nevertheless ferociously criticized yet with no visible reference to conflicts of the day. Daumier's heart-breaking vision well appears to correspond to reality, for there is a remarkable convergence—we will see this in the plates—between his observations in lithographic form and those which chroniclers, journalists, and physiologists of everyday life were offering in ever increasing numbers in print. In the first place, teachers supplied the caricaturist with a sadly rich range of human derelicts. The unfortunate supervisors especially inspired his verve. He portrayed them as old or ageless, poor and repugnant. The most frightening is perhaps the one in plate 8 asleep in his chair, nose dripping and wearing a frock-coat which might have been found in a dustbin. What we have here is a social wreck, a poor wretch who along with the study master is described in *les Français peints par eux-mêmes*. "He will blame the vicissitudes of fate for his wasted career and will be careful not to suggest any lack of merit, which alone has led him to this extreme condition. He is apathetic, heavy, inert; he will gladly doze off in his chair . . . a poor, suffering, painful soul, he is constantly being mocked by his pupils and reprimanded by his superiors." The supervisor in plate 5 is being hit in the eye by a snowball. "He is the target," states the same work, "of all children's pitiless pranks. 'I bet you,' says one, 'that I can hit him smack in the back' . . . No sooner said than the snowball is sailing swiftly through the air and strikes its goal. 'Oh, sir, I didn't do it on purpose,' the child exclaims, 'it's what's-his-name I was aiming at, but he moved!' Then he turns away and laughs into his cape while the poor man is obliged to be satisfied with this excuse." When he leaves the school with his pupils to take them for a walk or to watch over them at play, the supervisor assumes a dignified air with his frock-coat and top hat—which it would be better not to look at too closely—for he must seem a credit to the institution to which he belongs (plate 16). It is truly the lowliest of professions, as Louis Huart says in the *Muséum parisien* (1841), "a mere farmyard dog." The author goes on, "I would rather be a bus driver or the fare

9

collector at the Pont des Arts (then a toll bridge) . . . than watch over some fifty youngsters of ten or twelve years old ever bent on rebelling against discipline and preferring by far may-bugs to the great men of Greece or Rome."

The fate of the teachers themselves is scarcely more enviable. Under the name *professeur* (teacher) the alphabetical list of contents in *les Français peints par eux-mêmes* notes "cf. *black-coated penury*." It is under this title that the various studies of teachers, public writers, musicians and so on are grouped. Certainly, the teachers in Daumier's drawings by no means appear to be bathed in opulence, but at least they have the respectability which befits their station, for they are dressed in black coats and ties, though in all probability they have to touch over with black ink every day the frayed folds that have worn bare with use. This was a well-known practice. These individuals often appear to be serious-minded and wearied, with long asinine faces and spectacles (plates 17 and 18), or else with closed and obtuse expressions, and an appearance of quintessential stupidity (plate 3). The view Daumier gives us corresponds with fair accuracy to the opinions of numerous academics of the time who harbour no illusions about their colleagues. Eugène Manuel, in 1847, defines the teacher as an "ill-bred pedant whose job it is to persecute little imbeciles, an indescribable, dehumanized being. Shaggy-haired, with his spectacles perched on his nose, his fingers are covered with ink stains and his face has a week's beard." Sarcey, anxious to change his career, observes for his part that "there is nothing more soul-destroying than teaching; you go to bed as a man of intellect, but to your surprise find yourself waking up an absolute blockhead." Scribe, in one of his plays, portrays the mentality of the teacher; speaking of a young man for whom no suitable occupation can be found, a character remarks, "Well, why not put him into school teaching?"

The pupils are well matched to their masters. Here too, Daumier took his characters from the reality he observed around him. Most of them are shown wearing smocks, for as H. Rolland *(loc. cit.)* observes, "the smock is the most usual garment worn by pupils in the lowest classes." These smocks reached to halfway down their thighs, and they wore a large belt round their waists. Only on "outings" do they wear an overcoat or a frock-coat and a top hat. But as soon as they are a bit older, at first-form stage in the secondary school, they stop wearing their smocks, like the pupils in plate 15 who wish to play the role of rhetoricians. Obstinately entrenched in their indolence and boredom, their day brightened by the thought of doing something forbidden or of playing a trick on their tyrant of a teacher, or even in open revolt, the schoolboys in Daumier's drawing are portrayed in characteristic situations. Some of these typical situations were also seized upon by writers contemporary with Daumier and the subject matter of his drawings is echoed in their character sketches, monographs and *physiologies*.

In plate 19, a host of may-bugs takes wing, with one of them landing on the teacher's nose. Exactly the same scene is described by Édouard Ourliac in his *Physiologie de l'Écolier* (1841)—in springtime, the schoolboy "builds up a stock of may-bugs during his walks, until he has a box full of them . . . then he spreads them all over the place, on his classmates' books, on their benches or even on their clothes . . . Brrr, a may-bug takes wing, then another, and a third and a fourth follow, and soon there is an absolute cloud of them and a horrible buzzing fills the classroom, like one of the Plagues of Egypt. The other thing is that these may-bugs, though the heaviest and most stupid of insects, always have sufficient malice to end up by landing on the teacher's nose." Meanwhile, H. Rolland notes that "while on the subject of schoolboys, I mustn't omit to make mention of one of their great passions which is the keeping of animals. They shut silkworms in little boxes, and have all the trouble of getting hold of mulberry leaves for them and preventing them from being confiscated by the supervisors . . . If such happy pursuits are denied to the pupil, he makes do with may-bugs, stag-beetles and various other horned insects." In Monsieur Delteil's class great ingenuity is likewise expended in order to keep silkworms.

Another great schoolboy habit is the clandestine reading of forbidden literature which they hide under their textbooks and notebooks. According to the captions to plate 22, the pupil is reading a novel by Paul de Kock. This prolific author of somewhat poor quality was widely read; but the schoolboy in Daumier's lithograph is being rather more than usually precocious here, for H. Rolland was speaking of fourth-form pupils when he remarked, "The novels of Pigault-Lebrun and Paul de Kock are devoured with rapture and dubious passages are relished to the core, the authors' reticence being amply compensated by the astonishingly fecund imagination of their schoolboy readers." An amusing drawing dating from the same period shows three boarders giving their orders to an obliging day-boy, the first asking for pills, the second a razor, with the third exclaiming, "Don't forget to bring me *Amant de la Lune* by Paul de Kock." Here, as in the case of H. Rolland's remark, the schoolboys in question are reaching adolescence, and can no longer be classed as kids. Elsewhere, the first-form pupils whom Daumier depicts smoking—or trying to smoke, rather—are also precocious (plate 15), for it was not till fourth form that H. Rolland sees boys practising such forbidden pastimes. "Some of them try to smoke tobacco leaves rolled in the greasy paper distributed in the schools . . . the catastrophic results inevitably exposed the guilty one."

Recourse to cheating when they have not done their homework is another traditional schoolboy activity. In plate 1 we see a pupil reading off the lesson with the connivance of a classmate wearing a dunce's cap who is sitting holding up his book at the foot of the teacher's desk.   Édouard Ourliac made a comparable observation when he wrote, "I knew a pupil who would tear out his page of Greek roots every day and stick it on the teacher's desk, where he could calmly read it safely hidden from the teacher's eye."   Another well-known practice among certain pupils at this period was to sell their schoolbooks during the course of the year in order to raise a little money without worrying about the consequences (plate 24).   Champfleury related that one of Monsieur Delteil's pupils "had sold his dictionaries by weight to a grocer in the town in exchange for various cooking ingredients."

PRIVATE EDUCATION

The way of life in schools was like this throughout the educational system, but Daumier devoted nearly a dozen of his plates especially to private schools. Private schools and boarding establishments were often a form of fraud which he had not failed to include in his *Cent et un Robert Macaire*.   In a merciless monograph entitled *Boarding-school Master* in *les Français peints par eux-mêmes*, Élias Regnault observes that "a boarding school is an asylum open to the weaknesses of parents who do not wish to see their sons submitted to the discipline of State schools, to the weaknesses of children who have been spoiled early in life by maternal mollycoddling, to the weaknesses of rickety minds which have fruitlessly tried all sorts of university education. It is the hospice for all the intellectual and moral debilities imaginable.   These infirmities are incurable, as no doctor can do anything for wounds that cannot be healed. For such invalids, a charlatan is necessary, the boarding-school master, despite his conscience, is obliged to fulfil the role . . . the truth is demanded of him, yet anything other than fabrications causes offense.   The boarding-school master lives by deceit." In other words, his job is the skilful exploitation of pupils and their families.

Plate 14, grotesque and sinister, shows us an overcrowded dormitory.   The food, which Monsieur Adolphe Chamouillard revolts against in plate 10, is monotonous and stodgy.   Louis Huart's character Robert Macaire, himself a boarding-school master, says in the novel of 1839, "Nothing can be more harmful to young people's health than filling up their stomachs when they have intellectual work to do.   I've already bought fifty bags of lentils, sixty sacks of potatoes and eighty sacks of beans.   This means . . . they'll never have to eat the same thing two days running."   By contrast, outward appearances are kept up with the greatest care to impress the boys' families and be a good advertisement for the establishment.   The uniform, for example, according to the caption of plate 25 was for the pupils at the Institution Pascareau, a hat which "made them look a little like Napoleon Bonaparte and very like the little vendors of *l'Époque!*" This was a new newspaper, under regular attack from *le Charivari*. Although publishing its (paid) advertisements, *l'Époque* had thought of the idea of giving its vendors a ridiculous cocked hat which Daumier had recently scorned in one of his lithographs.

The main way, however, by which these establishments impressed their clientele was to make solemn play of the success they claimed for themselves. A cunning businessman, the head master was in the habit of offering scholarships to the parents of gifted children. "Every year they look up the list of prize winners in the general competitive exam," notes Élias Regnault, "and then they inquire into the social situation of the parents and waste no time in visiting those whose means are modest and offering to give their son a free place in their establishment." By this means, the institution is sure of winning distinctions which it has no hesitation in exploiting. "Their reputation is built up by the industrious children of the poor." Greluchot, the pupil in plate 27, is probably one such scholarship boy; with the fourteen prizes won at the Institution Bilboquet, the headmaster can proclaim in all the newspapers that it is the finest school in Paris.

But at the same time, the duffer sons of more moneyed parents must not be discouraged. To return to Élias Regnault, "There is not a mother, not even a father who does not hold his teacher responsible if their son is unsuccessful; so they must be made successful." Monsieur Alfred Cabassol wins the Cross of Honor, he is told in the caption of plate 6, because "you are the only one in the class not to have wiped your nose on your sleeve all week." This opinion is shared by Robert Macaire. "Displease the parents? Never! Impossible! Give prizes to everyone, give everyone his own!" Thus Monsieur Jean-Joseph Chaboulard, whose cretinous young profile lets out little hope, will at least get the first prize for good health (plate 28). Regnault notes that the headmaster in these boarding schools is careful to put on a prize-giving with a certain degree of pomp, intended to emphasize the brilliance of the prize-winners' achievements. Red bedspreads are unfolded as makeshift tapestries. If his speech is not a "literary work of outstanding merit, it is nonetheless a remarkable product. With great adroitness, he exploits in turn all the tender phrases calculated to warm the cockles of the maternal heart, and the pompous apostrophes to play up paternal vanities." Seeing his son showered with awards, Monsieur Cabuchet in plate 12 "can no longer hold back his tears of tenderness."

There is nothing to bring about the end of all these abuses. True, the Ministry sends out inspectors to private institutions, but though their visit is unannounced, everyone is at once warned of their arrival. "A messenger is advised of the inspector's arrival by a wink," we are told in the article entitled *les Examinateurs* in *le Prisme*, "and he quickly spreads the news throughout the establishment. The calamity is soon known everywhere; every frightened pupil conceals his illicit magazines, comics, novels, under a pile of books, behind respectable looking dictionaries . . . Everyone grabs some schoolbook or other and a pen . . . The inspector arrives and is impressed by the silence reigning in the classroom and the activity of all the pupils." With entire confidence the headmaster can then assure him that "perfect order reigns in my establishment" (plate 23). Even the food looks as though it leaves no room for improvement, for when the inspector goes down to the kitchen "a delicious smell regales his nostrils from afar. The pupils come and sit down to the banquet, and to their utter surprise are served with unaccustomed dishes instead of the usual lamb and the constant mutton with black sauce, mashed potato and beans," the same beans of which Monsieur Chamouillard complains. "The inspector leaves the kitchen," concludes *le Prisme*, "and bows to express his entire satisfaction . . ." Boarding schools have a long life ahead of them yet.

At the same time as it was publishing *Teachers and Students, le Charivari* published the following advertisement, "The Blanodet-Darragon Institute last year presented thirteen pupils for the *baccalauréat ès lettres*, and they all obtained their diploma, resounding confirmation of the scholastic excellence of the establishment."

If Daumier criticizes—and with what bitterness!—certain ridiculous or hateful aspects of school life, he seems little concerned with the contents of the teaching itself. In plates 17 and 18, the caricaturist appears to be denouncing the useless nature of the kind of knowledge children are obliged to learn by heart, useless because it is remote from life and everyday experience. A pupil who is unable to recite the names of the three sons of Dagobert is told "You don't know a thing, you seem determined to remain socially useless all your life!" And in an astronomy lesson, the pupils are recommended to take particular interest in the planet Saturn, because they are told, "You'll quite probably never have the opportunity in your whole life to observe it!" But we must not forget that in most cases Daumier is not the author of the captions of his plates. The title page of the smaller edition of *Cent et un Robert Macaire* (1839) bears the statement, "composed and designed by Monsieur H. Daumier after the ideas and captions of Monsieur Charles Philipon." Normally it is the reverse, the artist making his drawing on the lithographic stone and leaving to others the job of finding the suitable caption, or some appropriate comment. What we can say with certainty is that in these plates he has presented us with teachers who seem totally lacking in vitality and even in intelligence, which augurs badly for the quality of their teaching.

In two further plates (29 and 31) he holds up to scorn the "accomplishments" or more correctly the way they are taught in schools. Robert Macaire regards them as being principally an additional source of revenue. "Are the 'accomplishments' to be paid as extras?" he is asked. "Of course," he replies. So pupils blow their lungs out playing instruments or sit dreaming in front of the academic drawings they have to copy. Music plays an important part in certain provincial schools sometimes because the director tries to form a band and organize pompous processions in the neighboring town, an excellent way to advertise his school; this is what happens in the school at Laon in the *Souffrances du Professeur Delteil*. Gymnastics are similarly presented in an unfavorable light in plate 7. Amoros, a Spanish colonel naturalized Frenchman, had founded a gymnasium in Paris during the Restoration and launched a campaign for physical education. But it remained traditional to scorn and mock the whole idea, for twenty years after Daumier's lithographs, a drawing by Cham shows a schoolboy painfully suspended from the horizontal bar, with the caption, "Oh! Oh! my arms are sore, I preferred it when we did Greek instead."

REPRESSION AND REVOLT

The question of punishment was one of the most important aspects of school life around 1845. Daumier dealt with the question in this series, showing no mercy for those who were responsible for inflicting it. He is not severe in his condemnation of the dunce's cap or the pulling of children by the ear, and in fact, the meaning of the drawing is uncertain, but the whip is obviously one of the most fearful of all the methods of torture available to the supervisor (plates 8 and 11). The use of the rod is eloquently denounced in plate 2; it had existed for several centuries. At the end of the 17th century, Richelet had defined this particular instrument of torture as "a length of wood or leather, flattened at the end like the palm of the hand, and which is held in the hand, with which Jesuits and other teachers strike pupils who have committed some small fault." Balzac, recalling his own memories of the Collège de Vendôme, speaks of it with horror, "the famous rod," he remarks in *Louis Lambert*, "played with honor its terrible role. It was the *ultima ratio Patrum*. When homework was forgotten, lessons imperfectly learnt, or vulgar pranks played on the teacher, the *pensum* (detention exercise) was enough, but when his self-esteem was offended, the master responded with his rod. Of all the physical tortures to which we were subjected, the most painful was that inflicted by that leather rod, about twice as thick as a finger, applied to our feeble hands with all the force and outrage the Régent could muster." Daumier's régent is seen holding up his menacing-looking rod; he is an old man, with an eye shade shielding his tired eyes, a faithful advocate of the "old method," as the caption tells us, but there is no doubt that he takes pleasure in punishing his pupils, for his expression is not devoid of a certain sadistic contentment.   The pupil's terror is amply expressed by his drawn features and the wringing of his hands, and the resentment which is building up inside him.   What a reprehensible way to teach children!

Solitary confinement (plate 20) is even worse.   In the boarding school where Delteil teaches, "the cell, beneath the first floor staircase, is a dark spot which opens into the classroom itself.   The only way light can penetrate is through a little spyhole in the door."   The cell in Daumier's drawing is perhaps less dark but it is no less grim a place.   The pupils, under the guard of the porter, were kept here behind locked doors for an afternoon or a whole day, in Balzac's time the period of detention could even be several weeks.   On the bare wall, the prisoner has drawn a caricature of his teacher brandishing the rod.

But pupils are not disposed to undergo passively such repressive discipline, no more than they accept the authority of the administration, the teaching that is inflicted upon them, or the life they have to lead.   The imprisoned schoolboy is seen sticking out an eloquent tongue at the concerned-looking adult who has come to look at him through the window.   Monsieur Moutonnet is seen cocking a snook at his teacher's back when the latter gives him a verb to copy out (plate 3).   Elsewhere, the same thing—in plate 23, the pupil is seen cocking an equally eloquent snook behind the headmaster while he is vaunting the merits of his establishment to the inspector.   The various tricks that pupils played on their teachers and supervisors (plates 1, 5, 8 and 11) are also forms of protestation.   This revolt culminates in the explosion of plate 4— with the greatest of glee, the children throw up everything into the air: books and notebooks, caps and dunce's caps, even the wig of their teacher who is left stammering with consternation.   This riot is obviously a means of liberation.   Even those who never resort to such extreme demonstrations, have at least available to them a spontaneous reaction which serves as an indictment of their teachers—they yawn.   During the astronomy lesson, a pupil in the foreground is yawning his head off (plate 18); during a "slightly tiresome walk," when they are strolling in pairs along streets they know only too well, the pupils are once again seen yawning, thus filling their lungs with fresh air, which is, after all, the purpose of the walk (plate 16). This kind of education and indeed the whole scholastic system are calculated to produce boredom.

DAUMIER'S TRUE MEANING

It is perfectly obvious that Daumier approves of all these expressions of revolt; he is decidedly on the side of the pupils.   His advocacy of natural freedom leads him to welcome the revenge that nature and liberty take on the arbitrary laying down of the law and the self-satisfied stupidity, not to speak of the triumphant fraud, which seem to be for him the essence of the teaching system at the time. One of his best plates is doubtless number 13 where we see a pupil with a stomach-ache asking a sleepy supervisor for permission to leave the classroom. In this elementary revolt of simple nature against the absurdity of the established order there is an almost revolutionary force. Youth rebels against the tyrannical stupidity of its elders and Daumier's pencil shows how right youth is. The fact that the artist's attitude is so, need not necessarily be taken to mean that he has precise political ideas, an ideological position, even less, as we have already pointed out, that he has the deliberate intention of participating in the current debate on the question. We are dealing here not with political caricature, but with the observation of morals; Daumier's fundamental views are obvious enough, but at an almost visceral level, at the temperamental level. He is not suggesting a series of demands to be made, a list of reforms, or a new educational system, and if he had wanted to do so, he would scarcely have chosen to deal with the educational question at the level of the lower classes in the school. No, his drawings are both more superficial and more profound. He examines mercilessly a limited number of significant scenes and, as usual, his irrepressible good sense keeps the whole question in proportion; his denunciation is not so much of the university as of basic inhumanity.

It cannot even be stated with certainty that he was interested in children for their own sakes. It was the values they incorporate, be they good or bad, that he wished to defend. 1846 was nonetheless the year of his marriage, and before that of the birth, just at the time when he was drawing his kids, of an illegitimate child, Honoré, on February 2, 1846. Fatherhood did not make him any more tender or compassionate; the faces of his schoolboys are in no sense angelic and they scarcely recall innocent childhood. These small versions of men already have a certain number of faults and vices which they will doubtless develop later on; stubbornness, stupidity, laziness and caddishness. Indeed, many of them are already men; as well as a certain number of childish expressions, so obviously authentic, his pupils often have adult faces. In seeking to give expression to his drawings he is led to mark their features and even to harden them, so that certain grimacing countenances are no longer childish in appearance. In plate 14 the pupils in their nightcaps (especially the first two) have frightful little faces of ageless gnomes. It is the same thing that we find in other series where he chose to portray children, the *Papas,* the *Bons Bourgeois* and others; he gives them, as has been well noticed, "features which are not in accord with their age . . . and a prematurely wizened expression." (Escholier, *Daumier,* Berger-levrault, 1965, p. 116.)

Sometimes, despite the lack of attention to and interest in the child as such, these lithographs are striking for their psychological reality and accuracy. Each of these scenes strikes us at once and appears totally convincing, to such a point that the gesture and the movements acquire an exemplary value. A political editor of *le Charivari,* seeing the imprisoned pupil sticking out his tongue in plate 20 which was published on March 23, 1846 saw an immediate analogy between the attitudes of the schoolboy to his master and that of the ministers to the Chamber of Deputies. Under the title *Governmental Childishness* published on March 31 he wrote, "During these last days in one of the drawings of a series in our newspaper entitled *Teachers and Students,* there was a roguish schoolboy who, placed in the school cell and wishing to show his teacher just what he thought of him, his reprimands and his punishments, gives him through the bars a highly bantering grimace. This could pass quite well for a scene from representative government, replacing the teacher by the deputies and the roguish schoolboy by the minister." Let us note in passing that the journalist only looked at the drawing cursorily; this prison has no bars but only a window, in this case open, where there appears the head of an adult, probably the master himself; the main thing is that he was aware of the dramatic force of this portrayal of schoolboy revolt.

In fact, the thing that emerges most forcefully from all these plates is their dramatic quality, and this is certainly one of the essential features of Daumier's genius. Each one of these scenes, upsetting the equilibrium, is invested with the movement of a dynamic aesthetic. Active life continues to take place under our eyes. These drawings are in no sense motionless pictures; they are moving syntheses which come to life as soon as we look at them. Theatre without words, with all the expressive eloquence of the mime. This was well noticed by Baudelaire, "first of all it is the idea that we become aware of. We look, and understand. The captions below his drawings serve no great purpose, because in general they could quite well do without them" (*Quelques caricaturistes français,* 1857). These captions are merely simple comments among others that the little action drama above them could inspire. It is therefore not surprising to learn that Daumier is credited with having said so himself in so many words, "The caption is useless . . . if my drawing means nothing to you, then it must be bad; the caption will not make it any better. If my drawing is good, you will be perfectly able to understand it yourselves, so what is the use of the caption?" (A. Alexandre, *Daumier,* Laurens, 1888.)

In fact, the scene is sufficient in itself, and its graphic language—which has not been studied enough—is immediately intelligible. If only by virtue of their height, adults appear as almost monsters within this childish world; the pupils' revolt is thus presented as the revenge of David on Goliath. It is to be noticed that all the plates without exception are horizontal; this presentation emphasizes the difference in height, and almost in nature, between pupils and teachers. The inspector and the boarding-school headmaster, drawn with their full height, take up the whole of the center of plate 23; they reign, with majesty and a security emphasized by the enormous stomach of the headmaster, over the little crowd of schoolboys seated on the right, with their backs bent: yet on the left we can see one of these oppressed creatures cocking a magnificent snook at the back of these two giants. In plate 18, the teacher, standing like an enormous wader-bird, bizarre and melancholy, dominates by his great height his fascinated or bored pupils. Elsewhere as in plate 16, scholastic discipline is expressed in this geometric manner, in the drawing of the schoolboys out on their stroll, by the straight line of their top hats: two by two the pupils are carefully ranged according to their heights, with the smallest in front; but they are dreaming or yawning, and the sacrosanct order is held up to comic derision in the broken line of the uneven array of their hats. To understand Daumier fully, it is necessary to be sensitive to these graphic elements which are everywhere in his work.

But we must go further and say that not only does the figurative scene have its own self-sufficient language, but that often the drawing is also sufficient in itself, beyond all political, ideological or moral reference. Is it then pure drawing? Yes, no doubt, so long as this term does not exclude figurative representation which remains of capital importance. From his experience as a sculptor, Daumier derived the sense of all three dimensions; his figures occupy space, and have also consistency. Above all, they have weight, and it is this weight especially which gives the figures their great consistency. Instead of floating vaguely on the page, they are weighed down with reality. Daumier, a master of black and white drawing, the poet of light and shadow, who was at that time, let it be remembered, turning more and more to painting, is becoming increasingly interested in mass and composition. *Teachers and Students* is not perhaps one of his greatest series, but these plates, freed from the political occupations which sometimes detract from the qualities of earlier work, seem when we have conducted a graphic analysis of them to be exciting evidence of his tireless search and his ever-developing genius.

RAYMOND PICARD

Detailed reference to texts and documents quoted or otherwise mentioned in this preface will be found in the Catalogue raisonné *at the end of the book.*

UN SERVICE D'AMI.

— A la bonne heure au moins . . . . vous n'êtes pas comme ce petit paresseux de Julien . . . . . vous savez votre leçon sur le bout de votre doigt!... — Vieux jobard va.....c'est sur le bout du mien qu'il la sait!...

(Cette réflexion philosophique mais hardie, n'est émise par Mr Julien, qu'a voix très basse .)

LA VIEILLE MÉTHODE.

– Ah! drôle, vous passerez donc toute votre vie à mettre des queues de papier au séant des mouches !.... avancez moi votre main tout de suite. et ne la retirez que quand je vous en octroirai la permission !....

COMME ON DEVIENT GRAND MATHÉMATICIEN.

– Mr Moutonnet, vous avez encore commis une erreur dans votre calcul... vous me copierez six fois le verbe : je me suis **trompé dans mon addition** !

(Mr Moutonnet, devenu furieux, réplique par des signes qui ne sont point algébriques.)

UNE ÉMEUTE.

—Po po po lisson !.... je vais dou dou....bler tous vos devoirs !.....—— De quoi des devoirs...... sous un gouvernement despotique c'est l'insurrection qui est le seul devoir !.....

Un surveillant obligé de fermer l'œil sur la conduite de ses élèves.

—M.ʳ Alfred Cabassol, seul de la classe vous avez passé toute cette semaine sans vous moucher sur votre manche, recevez ce **signe de l'honneur sans tache** !.....

PROFESSEURS ET MOUTARDS.

Comme quoi la gymnastique forme les membres, mais déforme le nez.

Un jeune homme pour qui rien n'est sacré.

Jeunes imprudens qui se laissent emporter par le point d'honneur et qui narguent les arrets de la Cour de Cassation.

– Monsieu Adolphe Chamouillard vous vous montrerez donc perpetuellement difficile pour la nourriture . . . . je vous le déclare, vous n'êtes qu'un Sybarite . . . . apprenez que les Spartiates mangeaient toute l'année du brouet noir . . . .

– Mais au moins c'était pas toujours des haricots rouges ! . . . .

Attends, attends.... j'te vas en donner moi du maitre d'école !...

Premier grand prix de mathématiques, Mᵣ Isidore Cabuchet, déja neuf fois nommé !. . . . . . .
(Mᵣ Cabuchet ne peut plus contenir les larmes d'attendrissement qu'inondent décidèment son nez paternel.)

M'sieu..... **M'sieu**..... **M'siiieu**..... christi que c'est tannant d'avoir la colique quand le Pion pionse !......

LE DORTOIR D'UN PENSIONNAT BIEN TENU.

– Attention... au premier coup que je frapperai dans mes mains vous poserez la tête sur l'oreiller, au second coup vous fermerez les yeux... au troisième coup vous vous endormirez tous.

Elèves de sixième voulant jouer aux rhétoriciens.

PROFESSEURS ET MOUTARDS.

Promenade hygiènique et sentimentale, légèrement embêtante, mais remplissant parfaitement son but qui est de faire respirer de l'air à pleins poumons.

LA LEÇON D'HISTOIRE.

– Comment, drôle, vous ne savez pas le nom des trois fils de Dagobert . . . . . mais vous ne savez donc rien de rien . . . . mais vous voulez donc être toute votre vie un être inutile a la société ! . . . . .

– Demain nous nous occuperons de Saturne .... et je vous engage d'autant plus à apporter la plus grande attention à cette planête que très probablement vous n'aurez jamais de votre vie l'occasion de l'apercevoir !..

Triste sort des professeurs dans les années fertiles en hannetons !

Comme quoi l'emprisonnement cellulaire ne produit pas toujours d'excellens résultats.

Ah! tu rapportes tout au maitre, toi..... eh! ben rapportes lui donc ce coup de poing là!...

— Je ne m'étonne plus si celui la se tenait tranquille.... et s'il lisait si longtemps dans son dictionnaire grec, il y avait fourré un roman de Kock.... ou allons nous, bon dieu, ou allons nous !....

– Vous voyez, monsieur, l'ordre le plus parfait règne dans mon établissement,... et ce que vous ne sauriez vous imaginer, c'est combien je suis arrivé à inculquer à ces jeunes élèves un profond sentiment de respect pour leur maître !...

Jeunes collégiens trop propres, et **lavant** jusqu'à leur dictionnaire latin.

Les elèves de l'institution Pascareau essayent un nouvel uniforme, qui a l'agrément de les faire ressembler un peu au grand Napoléon et beaucoup à des petits porteurs de l'Epoque !....

Comment on décide un jeune homme à venir enfin rendre ses hommages respectueux à ses parens.

-Dans cette réclame que vous allez envoyer à tous les journaux, ne faites pas de charlatanisme... dites tout simplement que notre élève Greluchot a remporté quatorze prix et que l'institution Bilboquet est décidément la première de Paris!...

— Monsieur Jean - Joseph - Chaboulard . . . . premier prix de santé ! . . . .

Un jeune homme en train d'acquérir ce que l'on est convenu d'appeler un art d'agrément.

Ce qui nous prouve que, dès le collège, les hommes ne cherchent qu'à se passer pardessus les épaules les uns des autres.

Mission pénible et délicate du professeur de dessin, c'est à lui qu'est réservée constamment la tâche difficile de redresser les tords et les travers de ses jeunes élèves !

— Rappelez vous tous que l'élève Cabassol est trop fort en thème pour que je souffre jamais qu'il soit molesté.....
je le prends sous ma protection immédiate..... au concours général il sera l'honneur de l'Institution Bilboquet!...

Bibliography

I. TEACHING IN 1845

Texts and documents of Daumier's period:

A. Rendu, *Code universitaire*. Paris, Hachette, 1846, in-8º.

Les Français peints par eux-mêmes, encyclopédie morale du dix-neuvième siècle. Paris, Curmer, 1841, 8 vols. in-4º. The eighth volume is entitled *le Prisme*. Abridged in: *Français*.
— In volume I, E. Nyon, *Le Maître d'études*, pp. 333-340;
— In volume II, H. Rolland, *L'Écolier*, pp. 134-144; E. Regnault, *Le Maître de pension*, pp. 153-160.
— In volume VIII, *Les Examinateurs*, pp. 25-30.

Ed. Ourliac, *Physiologie de l'écolier*. Paris, Aubert, 1841, in-18. Abridged in: Ourliac.

L. Huart, *Muséum parisien, Histoire physiologique, pittoresque, philosophique et grotesque de toutes les bêtes curieuses de Paris et de la banlieue*. Paris, Beauger, 1841, in-8º. *Le chien de cour*, pp. 180-186.

Champfleury, *Les Souffrances du Professeur Delteil*. Paris, Rothschild, 1869, in-8º (first edition, 1853). Abridged in: Champfleury.

Histoire populaire contemporaine de la France. Paris, Lahure, 1865, 2 vols in-4º.

Studies:

P. Gerbod, *La Condition universitaire en France au XIXe siècle*. Paris, 1965, in-8º (thesis).

La Vie quotidienne dans les lycées et collèges au XIXe siècle. Paris, Hachette, 1968, in-12.

Catalogue raisonné

*T*he lithographic stones on which Daumier drew, delivered to him in numerical order, tell us the exact date of their production. The printing of the plates was done by the publisher Aubert, Philipon's brother-in-law, editor of le Charivari. Aubert deposited a copy of each at the Bibliothèque du Roi, where it was registered in numerical order with, so far as the lithographs which interest us here are concerned, the indication of the month and year. The plates in the series Teachers and Students *were published irregularly in* le Charivari *from December 2, 1845 to June 11 1846, with the exception of plates 18, 28, 30 and 32. They are numbered in the series in the order of their deposit at the Bibliothèque du Roi, but not in the very haphazard manner of their publication in* le Charivari. They are of course included in the Catalogue *by Hazard and Delteil. For each of them two states are mentioned, the first before the printed text, the second with the printed text, and it is always the second state that is here reproduced from the print in the Cabinet des Estampes which—contrary to the lithographs in* le Charivari *likewise in the second state—has no printed text on the other side. These plates are obviously included also in* le Peintre-graveur illustré *by Delteil.*

For each of the thirty-two lithographs studied in the following pages in the order of the series, we will find in turn the number of the stone, the dimensions in millimetres (width and height), the date of deposit at the Bibliothèque and the order number, the publication date in le Charivari *and the number of the newspaper, and finally the number in the* Catalogue *by Hazard and Delteil and in* le Peintre-graveur illustré *respectively. We thought it unnecessary to repeat the indications concerning the states which are valid for all the plates. The abbreviations are those listed in the bibliography on the following pages.*

Notes

1. A FRIENDLY SERVICE.

No. 833. 241 × 184 mm. Deposited in November 1845 (No. 3,563). Published in *le Charivari,* December 2, 1845 (No. 338). Unsigned. H.-D., No. 2,413. Delteil illustrated, No. 1,438.

The stones corresponding to the first four plates of the series were delivered together to Daumier (829-833); the first three lithographs were deposited at the same time at the Bibliothèque Nationale: they are of the same impetus and the fourth closely follows.

The relationship between the teacher and pupils is defined in space by the distance between the desk and the class. More than one-quarter of the lithographs of the series represents a desk, with the small lectern on which the teacher places his book. This teacher is rather aloof and absorbed in the lesson which the pupil is reading aloud to him. Thus it is rather unlikely that he notices the trick the two youngsters are playing on him. On similar ruses, see the Preface, p. 11, and Ourliac, pp. 80-81 (the scene inspired a vignette by Gavarni, *ibid*, p. 81). The best constructed drawing is that of the pupils standing, his head slightly bent in order to read the book which his comrade his holding open to him. The latter's dunce's cap, consisting of written pages, is a somewhat complicated affair. A similar cap is seen in plate 4.

The light falls directly on the three figures, with the amusing shadow of the dunce's cap on the front of the desk. In the half-light, on the left, drawn in a sketchy manner are two pupils, seated on benches and facing each other. In the entire series the pupils are shown in such a manner seated at long tables on which they are working; the seats are always benches, even at lunch (plate 10), except during the drawing course (plate 31) where the pupil is entitled to a chair.

2. THE OLD METHOD.

No. 829. 253 × 188 mm. Deposited in November 1845 (No. 3,564). Published in *le Charivari,* December 8, 1845 (No. 344). Signed H. D. H.-D., No. 2,414. Delteil illustrated, No. 1,439.

The stone is that which for this series has the oldest number, and it is not impossible that this plate may have been the first. Daumier would therefore have begun with this picture, significant to him, of the relationship between teacher and pupil. Indeed, in his eyes the teacher seems to have been above all the man with the cane. On this instrument, see the Preface, p. 15, the article *férule* in Richelet's *Dictionnaire, Louis Lambert* by Balzac (1822) published by Gallimard, Bibliothèque de la Pléiade, Volume X, p. 375.

The large threatening figure of the teacher dominates the scene, his right hand holding the cane in the air ready to strike, a vision children will never forget. Note that in plate 20 the drawing on the wall made by the rebellious prisoner shows a teacher holding a cane in a similar manner. A rather elderly person, he is wearing a kind of black bonnet similar to that shown in plate 13; his glasses on the tip of his nose and, in addition, his eyes are protected by an eye shade. The caption indicates that this personage prides himself on a ridiculous, old-fashioned respectability: "*au séant des mouches,*" "*je vous en octroierai la permission,*" but this interpretation appears arbitrary. On his slightly sadistic expression, see the Preface, p. 15.

The schoolboy represents a remarkable achievement from the point of view of psychological expression: contracted eyebrows, pursed lips, which indicate frustrated tears, twisted hands, all indicating apprehension and terror, and in addition a surly, obstinate air. This is a real "propaganda drawing," a revengeful condemnation of the *old method.*

In the background two children are studying and copying writing models outlined on large sheets of paper held by clips on a stretched piece of wire. The furnishings are plain and poor, the planks of the desk badly jointed.

3. HOW ONE BECOMES A MATHEMATICIAN.

No. 831. 250 × 196 mm. Deposited in November 1845 (No. 3,565). Published in *le Charivari,* December 15, 1845 (No. 315). Signed H. D. H.-D., No. 2,415. Delteil illustrated, No. 1,440.

The plate is divided equally in width between two conflicting figures: the teacher who is writing on the blackboard and, behind him, Monsieur Moutonnet, who is cocking a snook at him. Since the figures are standing, Daumier had to increase the height of this plate, which is almost 2 cm. more than the following one.

Stiff and dignified, the teacher has a spiteful look in his eye, a beaked nose, thin lips and a weak chin, his physiognomy expressing severity and a narrow mind. Monsieur Moutonnet has cruel features and a pointed nose. Overcome by a kind of mental exaltation, not only does he cock a snook at the teacher with his left hand but also raises the right one behind his head in mockery (compare this to the gesture in plate 23). The other schoolboys, in the shadow of the background, are partly hidden by their comrade. The large face seen above Moutonnet's right arm is scarcely childish.

4. A RIOT.

No. 832. 255 × 178 mm. Deposited in November 1845 (No. 3,588). Published in *le Charivari,* December 20, 1845

(No. 356). Unsigned. H.-D., No. 2,416. Delteil illustrated, No. 1,441.

Liberating explosions similar to this one were rather frequent in school life over which a fussy discipline hung heavily. An example is found in Champfleury, pp. 174-175. On the significance of this scene for Daumier, see the Preface, p. 16. He returned to this theme a few years later but treating the following phase, that of repression. The lithograph, the last of the *Papas* series (plate 23), is entitled *les Suites d'une insurrection*. It represents a schoolboy on his knees in the midst of the class, wearing a dunce's cap. Standing beside him is his father who, according to the caption, is saying to him, "Wretched boy, this is where your anarchist ideas have led you . . . You cried out: 'Down with grammar and junior masters!' I curse the day I brought you into this world." The *anarchist ideas* obviously evoke the atmosphere of the Second Republic, in fact the plate appeared in *le Charivari* on June 1, 1849.

Refusal and freedom are expressed on the entire width of the plate by a vertical movement. The force of this movement is made clear in all the accessories and attributes of school life symbolically thrown into the air. In addition, it is incarnated by the schoolboy with his back to us and both hands raised in the air and repeated in the brandished rulers. The teacher standing, with a stupid expression and mouth open, makes a frightening gesture. A schoolboy, behind him, uses his ruler to push up his wig. He holds his ruler in his left hand —which is strange, if he is not left-handed, but it gives Daumier an occasion to offer a charming attitude sketch. The puffy faces of the other pupils, on the right, are less successful.

5. A MASTER ON DUTY FORCED TO CLOSE HIS EYE . . .

No. 839. 246 × 188 mm. Deposited in December 1845 (No. 3,708). Published in *le Charivari*, December 24, 1845 (No. 360). Unsigned. H.-D., No. 2,417. Delteil illustrated, No. 1,442.

This plate inaugurates a cycle of this series, it follows the preceding ones by several weeks and was deposited as well as the six following ones—but a few days earlier—during the month of December at the Bibliothèque Nationale. For Christmas Daumier offered the *Charivari* readers a snow scene. The four preceding lithographs were interior scenes. This, on the contrary, take place in the school courtyard.

The master on duty, a corpulent giant dressed in a black frock-coat, fills a good part of the lithograph with his dark mass. Here again we find the Goliath theme (see the Preface, p. 19). The children rush forward excitely in the lower section, delimited horizontally almost on the level of the master's elbow. Snowballs are flying in all directions, explaining the accident which is the subject of the plate—but it is perhaps not a matter of chance (see *le Maître d'études, Français,* vol. 1, pp. 336-337). The children are simply sketched in a manner to compose a crowd, attention being on the victim, whose reactions are pleasantly exaggerated: backward motion, raised arm, open mouth, deformed face, hat falling behind, the snowball crushing him like a star of light.

6. MONSIEUR ALFRED CABASSOL, YOU ARE THE ONLY ONE IN THE CLASS NOT TO HAVE WIPED YOUR NOSE ON YOUR SLEEVE ALL WEEK . . .

No. 845. 242 × 182 mm. Deposited in December 1845 (No. 3,783). Published in *le Charivari*, January 10, 1846 (No. 10). Unsigned. H.-D., No. 2,418. Delteil illustrated, No. 1,443.

The number in the series does not correspond to the publication order in *le Charivari*, where plates 7, 9 and 10 appeared before this one. Yet all these lithographs, including plate 8, are contemporary and were deposited together at the Bibliothèque Nationale in December 1845.

Master and pupils are distributed equally on the surface of the plate. The master, on the right, looking very serious, bends over to pin a huge cross of honor on Monsieur Alfred Cabassol, who, standing in the first row of his comrades, modestly lowers his eyes. Prepared for this ceremony, he is the only one not wearing a blouse. Two pupils, on the left, appear rather dissatisfied and unconvinced of their comrade's merits.

The scene takes place at the far end of a perfectly blank wall.

Daumier often returns in this series to the theme of necessary and absurd rewards in private institutions, see plates 12, 27 and 28.

7. HOW GYMNASTICS FORM THE LIMBS BUT DEFORM THE NOSE.

No. 834. 243 × 195 mm. Deposited in December 1845 (No. 3,782). Published in *le Charivari*, December 27, 1845 (No. 362). Unsigned. H.-D., No. 2,419. Delteil illustrated, No. 1,444.

On gymnastics in school, see the preface, p. 15. The master on duty (or the gymnastics teacher?), a tall, black silhouette, stands in the center of the design and is wearing a black *calotte*. His expression appears to be one of concern and displeasure. Hands behind his back—the classic attitude of the master on duty—he is bent slightly towards two young pupils, one of whom is facing him. The features of this boy are clearly drawn in contrast to the sketchy ones of his seven comrades there to form a group.

The master on duty is not concerned with the mishaps of gymnastics, the subject of the plate illustrated by the three pupils represented in a kind of circumference around him. The first, hanging by one arm from a cord, views the ground with a frighted look: he is about to let go. The second is on the point of falling from the bar behind. The third, who has probably just fallen, is resting against a tree and, just behind the master on duty, is letting blood flow from his nose.

The layout is remarkable, the three figures forming an arabesque around the master on duty, his head fitting exactly into the angle formed by the bar and the supporting pole.

8. A YOUNG MAN FOR WHOM NOTHING IS SACRED.

No. 837. 248 × 191 mm. Deposited in December 1845 (No. 3,786). Published in *le Charivari*, January 18, 1846 (No. 18). Unsigned. H.-D., No. 2,420. Delteil illustrated, No. 1,445.

The scene is part of the traditional repertory of tricks played by pupils on their master on duty. But the trick itself is original. A pupil takes advantage of the sleeping man to approach him on tiptoe and to pull from beneath the collar of his frock-coat a kind of stiff cardboard band covered with material. The use of this object is not clear and may serve to give some style to the sloppy collar of this sordid clothing.

The central figure forms one of the most violent satires of the entire series. On the masters on duty, see the Preface and in *les Français* (vol. I, pp. 333-340), the monograph of *le Maître d'études* by E. Nyon. The sleeping master on duty is a human outcast with, as Daumier has drawn him, a truly frightening face. Before him on the small lectern, quite evident, is his working instrument, namely, the whip. Alongside the inkwell is an object which may well be a rag or handkerchief. Actually, it is probably a pair of socks or soft slippers which the master on duty may have removed to feel more at ease.

The pupil, "for whom nothing is sacred," is wide awake, his attitude is attentive and at the same time concerned; his left hand is resting on the back of the chair in order to have a lighter right hand and succeed in the delicate act.

The group of his comrades, sketched casually on the left, is less successful. The feeling of curiosity and amusement as well as of fear is well expressed, but the faces are too massive and the features too marked here to be those of children.

9. RASH YOUNG PUPILS FIGHT OVER A POINT OF HONOR IN DEFIANCE OF THE RULES . . .

No. 843. 246 × 191 mm. Deposited in December 1845 (No. 3,785). Published in *le Charivari*, December 30, 1845 (No. 364). Signed H. D. H.-D., No. 2,421. Delteil illustrated, No. 1,446.

In the school playground two schoolboys are fighting, surrounded by their comrades; the master on duty sees them and approaches.

The drawing is especially remarkable for the sketches of movement. One of the boys fighting, furious, has seized his adversary by the hair. The latter, paralysed by pain, seems incapable of striking. Two schoolboys, left and right, are violently moved and in imitation or because they are about to intervene their arms are outstretched. We can see or guess four other heads, more or less sketchily indicated, which are there to complete the group. Above and behind this mass which occupies horizontally half the plate appears the master on duty wearing the eternal black *calotte*. He advances anxiously, for children are forbidden to fight and the responsibility is his.

10 MONSIEUR ADOLPHE CHAMOUILLARD, YOU ARE AS FUSSY AS EVER ABOUT YOUR FOOD . . .

No. 838. 247 × 195 mm. Deposited in December 1845 (No. 3,784). Published in *le Charivari*, January 5, 1846 (No. 5). Unsigned. H.-D., No. 2,422. Delteil illustrated, No. 1,447.

Here again the large dark figure of the master on duty dominates the scene, and all the more so as the children are seated at the table. The man is younger than his colleagues and dressed in a less careless way. Perhaps Daumier wished after all to represent a *maître de pension*, but in this case it would be rather strange for him to serve the boarders himself at the table and have their dishes passed. His face, with raised eyebrow and fixed look, expresses surprise and reprobation. While he passes the dish to the right, arms and body turned in this direction, his head is turned to the left, giving a feeling of vivacity. The figure is about to reply to a sudden remark made by Monsieur Chamouillard.

The pupils are prudently seated and Daumier has achieved in the foreground two charming attitude sketches. Of the two schoolboys with their backs to us, the one is looking at the teacher and the other, his head sunk into his shoulders, appears to have begun to eat. Monsieur Chamouillard, seated at the far end of the table, on the left, has a questioning and demanding look, but here again his is a man's face on the body of a child.

On the food in the *pensions*, see the Preface, p. 12, and the text by Huart in issue *32* of the *Cent et un Robert Macaire* (Paris, Aubert, 1839).

11. NOW THEN . . . I'LL GIVE YOU SOME OF THE TEACHER'S MEDICINE . . .

No. 849. 245 × 186 mm. Deposited in December 1845 (No. 4,072). Published in *le Charivari*, January 26, 1846 (No. 26). Unsigned. H.-D., No. 2,423. Delteil illustrated, No. 1,448.

Another pupils' offensive in the war between students and junior masters. In a kind of coup d'état—but very temporary—a schoolboy occupies the junior master's armchair in the very center of the plate. In his left hand is the whip, symbol of the authority that he usurps, he is wearing the cap and, on the tip of his nose, the junior master's glasses. To amuse his comrades, he is acting a part in their presence and assumes a dominating air.

In relationship to him in the background, two masses balance each other in the foreground and in the far plane: that of the junior master who, having stepped out of the classroom, returns and sees the sight. He is represented in the extreme foreground on the right, huge and threatening. He is about to open the door. He is a man of middle age, tired, sloppy (his frock-coat is unbuttoned) and does not seem to understand the joke.

Symmetrically, the group of children farthest away gaze upon the scene with varied feelings. Two of them in the front row burst out laughing, but two others, behind them, have caught sight of the junior master, and the expression of the schoolboy on the left is one of terror.

The background, from which the central figure emerges, consists of a kind of screen destined perhaps to protect the junior master from draughts.

12. FIRST GRAND PRIX IN MATHEMATICS, MONSIEUR ISIDORE CABUCHET, CITED NINE TIMES ALREADY ! . . .

No. 853. 237 × 182 mm. Deposited in January 1846 (No. 14). Published in *le Charivari*, February 16, 1846 (No 47). Unsigned. H.-D., No. 2,424. Delteil illustrated, No. 1,449.

On the "industrial" importance of rewards and prizes, especially in private teaching, ses plates 6, 27 and 28 of the present series. See also the Preface, p. 13 as well as Élias Regnault, *le Maître de pension*, in *les Français*, vol. II, pp. 157-159.

The two centers of interest of this plate are, on the left, the young Cabuchet receiving a crown and, on the right, in the foreground, his father shedding tears of emotion.

In the room pompously hung with draperies (the red foot-covers of the pupils' beds?), young Cabuchet, who cannot be more than seven or eight, is standing, his back to us, on a small platform, facing the desk, and the *maître de pension* (or the personality presiding over this distribution of prizes) offers him a fresh crown. Note Daumier's correction over the right shoulder of this figure.

The father, overcome with emotion, is unfolding a handkerchief, while tears are flowing over his large nose. The mass of pupils' parents is simply sketched. To avoid repetition, Daumier has hidden under a large hat the face of Monsieur Cabuchet's neighbor (Madame Cabuchet?).

13. SIR! . . . PLEASE, SIR! I SAY, SIR! . . . GOD, IT'S AWFUL TO BE SUFFERING FROM COLIC WHEN THE SUPERVISOR IS SUPERVISING!

No. 855. 255 × 180 mm. Deposited in January 1846 (No. 15). Published in *le Charivari*, January 30, 1846 (No. 30). Unsigned. H.-D., No. 2,425. Delteil illustrated, No. 1,450.

This lithograph, the preceding and the following one were deposited together at the Bibliothèque Nationale. The number in the series continues not to correspond to the publication order in *le Charivari*.

Here again it is a matter of an impossible dialogue between students and junior masters. The two interlocutors face each other and are separated symbolically by the pulpit.

The pupil with colic forms a wonderful expression sketch. A frighted look, tight lips, he raises his left hand in a desperate movement for permission to leave the room, while his right hand is on his stomach. The bent right leg gives a sharp feeling of the poor lad's pain. Note Daumier's correction which originally seems to have placed the left arm more vertically.

The junior master is sprawled in his chair, head bent forward and arms crossed. He has pushed his glasses on his black bonnet. He is an elderly man without the repulsive aspect of the sleeping junior master of plate 8 to whom he must be compared.

The pupils sketched on the left are plunged into their work and are unconcerned with the drama taking place.

Here we have an elementary revolt of nature against an oppressive and stupid system. This splendid lithograph certainly forms one of the most efficient protests of the entire series (see the Preface, p. 16).

14. THE DORMITORY OF A WELL-KEPT BOARDING SCHOOL.

No. 856. 253 × 180 mm. Deposited in January 1846 (No. 16). Published in *le Charivari*, February 3, 1846 (No. 34). Unsigned. H.-D., No. 2,426. Delteil illustrated, No. 1,451.

This nocturnal scene against a dark background, again sets junior master and students face to face. Of the junior master, a section of white drawn from the half-light, we see nothing more than an angular face and the hands which he is ready to strike to give some absurd signal.

The pupils in the foreground, ranged three in a bed, are ridiculously dressed with their pointed nightcaps.

Daumier seems to have sacrificed everything to the burlesque vision and to the pleasure of denouncing an aberrant discipline. There is nothing childish in the faces, and the pupils would be incapable of stretching out on the much too short bed on which the caricaturist has seated them.

15. PUPILS WISHING TO PLAY THE ROLE OF RHETORICIANS.

No. 852. 232 × 186 mm. Deposited in January 1846 (No. 95). Published in *le Charivari*, February 9, 1846 (No. 400). Signed H. D. H.-D., No. 2,427. Delteil illustrated, No. 1,452.

Daumier presents two amusing *physionomies* of novice smokers, while in the center a third pupil turns towards his comrades while lighting his pipe. All three are wearing fine uniforms, frock-coat and black tie, but to persuade themselves that they are really "grown up," they must try to smoke.

The first, on the right, stands fully straight and draws on his pipe, assuming a superior air. The second, on the left, is about to light his pipe; in his left hands he still holds a piece of amadou; his cheeks become hollow as he inhales and this, with his elongated aspect, gives his face a particularly comic expression.

On tobacco in the boarding school and its "deadly results," see H. Rolland, *L'Écolier* in *les Français*, vol. II, p. 143. L'Huart in *le Chien de cour* (*Muséum parisien*, p. 182) notes: "The schoolboy considers himself quite the young man the day he smokes for three minutes without feeling completely nauseated."

16. A SLIGHTLY BORING BUT UNDOUBTEDLY HEALTH-GIVING STROLL . . .

No. 2. 248 × 187 mm. Deposited in January 1846 (No. 213). Published in *le Charivari*, February 23, 1846 (No. 54). Unsigned. H.-D., No. 2,428. Delteil illustrated, No. 1,453.

With this plate begins a fresh series of lithographic stones which strangely enough, end with the following plate. In fact, the old series begins again with plate 18.

In an only slightly sketched urban décor, seven pupils are strolling under the watchful eye of a junior master. On the descending line which rules the composition as well as the

broken line formed by the three top hats in the foreground, see the Preface, p. 18 and on the yawning, p. 16.

The junior master, who wishes to honor his school, has a dignified air. As for the pupils, some are yawning and others, the first on the right, for example, appear to be walking in their sleep.

17. THE HISTORY LESSON.

No. 3. 247 × 175 mm. Deposited in January 1845 (No. 212). Published in *le Charivari*, March 3, 1846 (No. 62). Unsigned. H.-D., No. 2,429. Delteil illustrated, No. 1,454.

Once again master and pupil confront each other and are separated by the desk. The face of the teacher, on the right, stands out against an entirely white background, while that of the pupil is against a grey background.

The teacher appears austere and annoyed. On this type of person, here and in the following plate, see the Preface, p. 10.

The expression of the pupil is remarkable, with his downcast look, head slightly bent, eyes closed, exactly the attitude of one who has "cut" a class.

All his comrades, one of whom, his back to us, are working in the background in the same arrangement as previously noticed.

18. TOMORROW WE WILL OCCUPY SATURN . . .

No. 846. 234 × 190 mm. Deposited in February 1846 (No. 322). Not published in *le Charivari*. Unsigned. H.-D., No. 2,430. Delteil illustrated, No. 1,455.

The lithographic stone, judging by its number, had been given to Daumier as early as December 1845. This stone was kept in abeyance and finally was not used in *le Charivari*. Moreover, publication of the plates in this series became increasingly irregular: three plates in March and three in April.

On the two rows which here again define this plate, see the Preface, p. 18.

The tall dark silhouette of the teacher stands out from the planisphere hanging on the wall. This figure is characterized by his lack of vitality. With his finger he is pointing to a celestial globe standing in the center of the table around which the children are grouped in the lower row.

Daumier has varied the expressions: great boredom in the pupil who is yawning in the foreground, amusement on the part of his neighbor on the left, having discovered something under the table to divert him, attentive expression on a few others.

19. SAD FATE OF TEACHERS IN THE VINTAGE YEARS FOR MAY-BUGS!

No. 868. 247 × 198 mm. Deposited in February, 1846 (No. 389). Published in *le Charivari*, March 15, 1846 (No. 74). Signed H. D. H.-D., No. 2,431. Delteil illustrated, No. 1,456.

On may-bugs in school life, see the Preface, p. 11 as well as *les Français*, vol. II, p. 139, and Ourliac, pp. 84-85. Here Daumier has adopted the same characteristic arrangement as in plates 13 and 17. The scene is systematically divided vertically into two zones: a light section with an entirely white background, against which the teacher stands out, and a rather dark section, with a grey background, where we find the pupils. This separation is rather unreal, and it is difficult to see how the white wall can suddenly emerge from the half-light, even if there is an angle. It is obvious that for Daumier this proved necessary to the composition and in turn a conventional means.

Thus used to its greatest effect, the silhouette of the teacher confronted by the may-bug is among the most amusing in the series. The personage straightens his back in the chair, hands before him, in the liveliest attitude of surprise. His eye is fixed on the may-bug, which has settled on the tip of his nose (compare this with the expression of the junior master in plate 5, struck by a snowball).

The group of children, on the right, watches with great interest the flight of may-bugs, who escape from a kind of bag lying on the table. A child with his back to us, the owner of the bag, raises his arms in the air to catch the fleeing may-bugs. The faces of the two children on the right are rather heavy. As for the may-bugs, their size has clearly been exaggerated and their representation is scarcely convincing.

20. BEING LOCKED IN A CELL DOES NOT ALWAYS PRODUCE THE BEST RESULTS.

No. 870. 251 × 197 mm. Deposited in February 1846 (No. 434). Published in *le Charivari*, March 23, 1846 (No. 82). Signed H. D. H.-D., No. 2,432. Delteil illustrated, No. 1,457.

On school prisons, see the Preface, pp. 15-16 and Champfleury, p. 178.

Teacher and child confront each other in a rather dramatic manner. Rebellion is expressed in the taut, stretched body of the schoolboy and of course in his convulsed face as he sticks out his tongue.

The person at the window is probably a teacher, though the somewhat soft face has a feminine aspect. He looks upon the prisoner with an anxious and grieved expression.

On the table against which the schoolboy is leaning are a book and a notebook covered with figures, pages torn out and a bird made out of folded paper, which shows that the prisoner was not concerned about the impositions given to him.

21. AH! YOU TELL EVERYTHING TO THE TEACHER, DO YOU . . . WELL THEN, TELL HIM ABOUT THIS PUNCH! . . .

No. 871. 250 × 198 mm. Deposited in February 1846 (No. 611). Published in *le Charivari*, April 3, 1846 (No. 93). Signed H. D. H.-D., No. 2,433. Delteil illustrated, No. 1,458.

This is the only outdoor country scene in the entire series, a kind of game played on the ground and very vaguely drawn.

The subject chosen is the punishment of a "squealer." He who is inflicting punishment, defender of the unwritten laws governing relationships among schoolboys, stands exactly in the center of the plate and offers an energetic action sketch. The entire force of his body is concentrated in the left fist, and the effort is everywhere expressed, down to the right fist.

The victim disappears beneath the squashed top-hat shoved down as far as his nose. All we see is his open mouth. No longer able to see, he places his hands in front of him, while his body cringes under the shock.

On the left, in the distance, other schoolboys are playing, hopping over one another or running under the watchful eye of the teacher or the junior master. He who has his back turned to the principal scene has observed nothing at all.

22. SO THAT'S WHY YOU ARE SO INTERESTED IN READING YOUR GREEK DICTIONARY — YOU HAVE A NOVEL HIDDEN INSIDE IT.

No. 872. 248 × 197 mm. Deposited in March 1846 (No. 704). Published in *le Charivari*, April 15, 1846 (No. 105). Signed H. D. H.-D., No. 2,434. Delteil illustrated, No. 1,459.

The supervisor dominates the scene and occupies the left part of the design, yet he is turned to the right. His expression is remarkable, body bent slightly backwards in order better to upbraid the pupil, his left hand eloquently showing the book held in his right hand, anxious brow, bitter expression around the mouth.

The schoolboy harangued in such a manner forms an excellent study (compare the pupils of plates 2 and 17). He lowers his head, arches his eyebrows, tightens his lips and has a obstinate look.

The text of the caption is not satisfactory and it is uncertain whether its author well understood the meaning of this lithograph. There is no sign on the table of the heavy Greek dictionary in which the pupil could easily have hidden his novel. In addition, are we certain it is a novel? Perhaps while busy at his homework, he was copying from the book. He may have made an error and turned to the book to correct it. One fact is certain: he is being violently scolded by the teacher.

The other pupils are slightly indicated, according to a horizontal which crosses the entire plate. In addition, at the same table as the hero, is an attractive sketch representing a schoolboy in the act of writing, yet actually very much aware of what is happening beside him.

23. YOU SEE, SIR, THE MOST PERFECT ORDER REIGNS IN MY BOARDING SCHOOL . . .

No. 880. 254 × 197 mm. Deposited in March 1846 (under the same number as the preceding plate). Published in *le Charivari*, May 6, 1846 (No. 126). Signed H. D. H.-D., No. 2,435. Delteil illustrated, No. 1,460.

On the composition and interpretation of this plate, see the Preface, p. 13. In their *Catalogue*, Hazard and Delteil believe this to be a pupil's parent, who is being shown through the *pension* by the master. According to documentary evidence of the period (cf. *le Prisme*, p. 29), it is more likely that the visitor is an inspector from the Ministry of Education. Moreover, he has the severe expression of an inquisitor: furrowed brow, oblique fold extending from the nose, thin lips.

The boarding-school master is the sole bourgeois in the Daumier manner whom we find in this university series: large, self-satisfied, rubicond expression, huge stomach, utterly different from every point of view from his interlocutor.

24. PUPILS WHO ARE SO CLEAN THEY EVEN "WASH" (FRENCH SLANG FOR "FLOG") THEIR LATIN DICTIONARIES.

No. 883. 243 × 190 mm. Deposited in March 1846 (No. 779). Published in *le Charivari*, May 14, 1846 (No. 134). Signed H. D. H.-D., No. 2,436. Delteil illustrated, No. 1,461.

This is the sole scene in which the schoolboys are represented turned over to themselves "in the great wide world," far from the watchful eye of the junior master. They take advantage of their freedom to sell one of their textbooks to a book dealer along the quay (on this habit see Champfleury, p. 130). The old Parisian houses which serve as background appear very close. Perhaps they are separated from the foreground merely by a branch of the Seine, as is the case, for example, between the Pont-Neuf and the Pont Saint-Michel. Against this picturesque background are three figures. Daumier has been very careful in portraying the bookseller, whose attentive expression and the look of an auctioneer are true to life. The two schoolboys on the right, rather ridiculous in their frock-coat buttoned to the neck and wearing top hats, anxiously await his decision.

25. PUPILS OF THE INSTITUTION PASCAREAU TRYING ON A NEW UNIFORM . . .

No. 886. 236 × 192 mm. Deposited in March 1846 (under the same number as the preceding plate). Published in *le*

Charivari, May 16, 1846 (No. 136). Signed H. D. H.-D., No. 2,437. Delteil illustrated, No. 1,462.

This lithograph, along with the preceding one, marks a new cycle in the series which Daumier finally decided to finish. Four plates in this series appeared one after another in *le Charivari* in a dozen days, while only two plates had appeared during the course of the previous month.

On the newspaper *l'Époque,* see the Preface, p. 12. It is uncertain whether Daumier had thought of this comparison with those who sold *l'Époque,* for the hat the latter wore was a cocked one pointed forward. On the publicity importance of the uniform for the colleges and boarding schools, see Champfleury, pp. 20-21, which describe a schoolboy parade in the wake of firemen from the city of Laon: "Enthusiasm was at its height when there appeared the cocked hats worn by the schoolboys, from the rhetorical students to those in second form. These two-pointed hats, made in the most mysterious manner by the hatter Vinson, received the honors of the review. The schoolboys, following the headmaster's instructions, did not wear their hats *broadside* after the fashion of gendarmes . . . more ingeniously the headmaster took his inspiration from the top hats worn by fashionable members of the Directory and naturally enlarged them so that one of the points cast a shadow on the pupil's nose and give them something of a military look. The commander of the National Guard and the *préfet* complimented the headmaster on the excellent dress of his pupils and on the majesty of their pointed hats." The hat tried on at the Institution Pascareau is here worn *broadside* after the fashion of Napoleon. The headdress in question, proudly worn by the chief figure, stands out against a white background. This absurd headdress, perched on the head of an unintelligent and serious student, produces the comical effect desired by Daumier. The schoolboy wearing the second hat is less of a caricature and slightly less ridiculous. Two other students in the background are lightly indicated.

On the left, the master, quite a young man still and dressed in a rather disgraceful frock-coat, appears to regard this vestimentary innovation with a perplexed eye.

26. How to persuade a young man to pay his respects to his parents.

No. 884. 248 × 188 mm. Deposited in March 1846 (No. 791). Published in *le Charivari,* May 19, 1846 (No. 139). Unsigned. H.-D., No. 2,438. Delteil illustrated, No. 1,463.

Here again the caption is unsatisfactory. It is not that the young man refuses to greet his mother; what we have here is a characteristic scene where the teacher leads a pupil guilty of some school misdemeanour to his mother so that she may severely scold him.

The expression of the boarding-school master in "bourgeois" dress, namely, frock-coat, white tie, tasselled cap, is precisely full of acid reprobation: eyes wide open and eyebrows so thin, they are little more than two vertical lines. Tugged by the ear by the central figure, the schoolboy comically expresses his helplessness with open hands outstretched and his face twisted. Facing him opposite the teacher is his mother reduced to an elegant silhouette, her features hidden by her capeline, the shawl emphasizing her shape.

The scene takes place in the school playground. Above the wall we can see the neighboring houses, as in plates 5, 7 and 9. Around a tree are four schoolboys lightly indicated.

27. In this publicity you are going to mail to every newspaper, don't do anything charlatan . . .

No. 887. 237 × 190 mm. Deposited in March 1846 (No. 818). Published in *le Charivari,* May 26, 1846 (No. 146).

Signed H. D. H.-D., No. 2,439. Delteil illustrated, No. 1,464.

On the publicity of private institutions, see the Preface, pp. 12-13.

Standing on the right, the boarding-school master dominates the scene by his advantageous silhouette. A satisfied bourgeois, bald and with flowing sideburns, he is proud of himself, turns his head back slightly, giving himself an air of disdainful authority, while he extends a protective left arm on Greluchot's shoulder and an imperative right arm towards his secretary. The distribution of prizes has just taken place and he is still dressed for the ceremony: white vest and white tie.

Thin Greluchot has the unattractive face and round forehead of the good pupil, his arms still loaded with palms. The secretary has his back turned to us. The setting is that of the schoolmaster's office with a world map hanging on the wall.

28. Monsieur Jean-Joseph Chaboulard . . . first prize in health ! . . .

No. 892. 243 × 191 mm. Deposited in March 1846 (No. 959). Not published in *le Charivari.* Unsigned. H.-D., No. 2,440. Delteil illustrated, No. 1,465.

On the importance of awards and the distributions of prizes in private institutions, see the Preface, p. 13.

One of the scenes of distribution of prizes is here included in the series. It was probably not published in *le Charivari* because it largely repeated plate 12. In fact, more generally speaking, it appears that Philipon, who already had sufficient material, was tired in the early summer of 1846 of school and university subject matter: of the five last plates in the series, three were not published in *le Charivari.*

If the idea and subject are the same, the composition here is quite different from the one in plate 12: no drapery and the schoolboy with his palms occupies the foreground.

Young Chaboulard, prematurely fat, has a hydrocephalic head, which really offers little assurance about his health. Here again the caption leaves much to be desired.

The teacher who is crowning him is yet another of Daumier's examples of the profession, and what comes forth most forcefully is the feeling of a timorous mind retracted to the point of stupidity.

The public—grandparents rather than parents—is indicated in a few well-drawn lines.

29. A young man about to acquire what is usually known as a pleasant air.

No. 891. 241 × 192 mm. Deposited in March 1846 (No. 958). Published in *le Charivari,* June 4, 1846 (No. 155). Unsigned. H.-D., No. 2,441. Delteil illustrated, No. 1,466.

On accomplishments in boarding schools, see the Preface, p. 14.

The figures are separated by the double music stand. On the right the teacher is about to scold his pupil, who appears incapable of producing on the clarine the note required of him. The pupil's clumsy effort is expressed not only in the puffed jowls but also in the fingers as though they were mere pieces of wood on the instrument. The teacher's expression is one of despair as well as of reprobation. Note that his curly hair and artistic air distinguish him from other music teachers.

On the left, a pupil wearing a smock and not a frock-coat like his comrade's, is about to blow into a saxhorn.

A painting on the wall seems to indicate that the lessons are being given in a drawing room and not, as with other courses, in a classroom.

MM. Kahan-Rabecq and L. Cros, *Un siècle d'enseignement à travers la caricature et l'image, 1805-1905*. Paris, 1952, in-8⁰ (catalogue of the exhibition at the Musée Pédagogique).

Louis-Grimaud, *Histoire de la liberté de l'enseignement en France*. Paris, Rousseau, in-8⁰. Volume VI (July Monarchy), 1954.

A. Prost, *L'Enseignement en France, 1800-1967*. Paris, A. Colin, 1968, in-8⁰ (Collection U).

II. THE LITHOGRAPHS BY DAUMIER

N.-A. Hazard and L. Delteil, *Catalogue raisonné de l'œuvre lithographié de Daumier*. 1904, in-4⁰. Abridged in: H.-D.

L. Delteil, *Le Peintre-graveur illustré*. Volumes XX and XXIX *bis* are devoted to Daumier, 11 volumes in-4⁰, 1926-1929. *Professeurs et Moutards* is found in volume XXIV (1926). Abridged in: Delteil illustré.

In the very extensive bibliography devoted to Daumier, there are relatively few serious studies devoted to the lithographs. Mention should be made of those works which have already appeared in the present collection by Jean Adhémar, Julien Cain, Henri Mondor, Philippe Roberts-Jones.

30. In which we see that, even as schoolboys, men learn to gain advancement by "leap-frogging" over the backs of others.

No. 890. 241 × 191 mm. Deposited in March 1846 (No. 957). Not published in *le Charivari*. Unsigned. H.-D., No. 2,442. Delteil illustrated, No. 1,467.

Like plate 21, these are outdoor games under the watchful eye of a junior master, who is portrayed standing, wearing a top hat and a frock-coat, his back turned to the pupils as he reads a newspaper.

The central figure is that of a student playing leap frog. His anxious look stems from the fact that perhaps on falling he will hit a comrade who, coming from the right, dangerously approaches him. The meaning of the activity of this figure represented with his head bent forward slightly, eyes closed and mouth open, is unclear; one would say he is about to sneeze, but actually he seems to be training for a race. Other than the sketch on the left, moreover, the drawing is rather unclear, and the figures are somewhat confused against a foliage background.

31. A drawing teacher's painful and delicate mission . . .

No. 848. 244 × 182 mm. Deposited in April 1846 (No. 1,117). Published in *le Charivari*, June 11, 1846 (No. 162). One can perhaps distinguish the signature H. D. in the left corner, but it remains very doubtful. H.-D., No. 2,443. Delteil illustrated, No. 1,468.

The last plate of the series which was published in *le Charivari*. The stone had been delivered to Daumier about six months earlier, and we assume that the artist put it aside after a first attempt which failed to satisfy him completely and to which he subsequently returned.

The drawing teacher, wearing a frock-coat and a black bonnet upon which he has raised his glasses, is standing, one hand on the back of the chair in which the pupil is seated, squinting as he measures the proportions of an academic drawing which acts as a model and which is attached by clips to a wire. The seated pupil stares at the model with a sad expression, holding before him his own drawing which is vaguely indicated.

The satirical significance, if any, of this lithograph is not clear. There are several ridiculous elements but none very striking.

32. Remember that pupil Cabassol is too good at book learning for me to tolerate his ever being bothered . . .

No. 879. 250 × 192 mm. Deposited in April 1846 (No. 1,118). Not published in *le Charivari*. Signed H. D. H.-D., No. 2,444. Delteil illustrated, No. 1,469.

On the industrial use of good pupils in private institutions, see the Preface, p. 13.

In this last plate, the teacher once again dominates the scene. Teacher or boarding-school master, this figure in a black frock-coat, battered forehead, potato-shaped nose, his hair ending in sideburns, extends a protective hand above the pupil in question and speaks to his comrades.

The hero of the scene, seated in the foreground, modestly lowers his eyes to his book, while his neighbor, without turning his head entirely, regards the speaker with a critical air. In contrast to these carefully indicated expressions, the other faces are only vaguely outlined.

THIS BOOK
DESIGNED AND COMPILED BY ANDRÉ
SAURET WAS FINISHED IN JUNE 1970.
THE TEXT WAS PRINTED BY THE IMPRI-
MERIE DARANTIERE AT DIJON.   THE
REPRODUCTIONS OF THE LITHOGRAPHS
WERE PRINTED BY THE IMPRIMERIE
MODERNE DU LION IN PARIS.

1970

U

242036